The Story of Our Holidays

HALLOWEEN

Joanna Ponto and Fay Robinson

Enslow Publishing
101 W. 23rd Street
Suite 240
New York, NY 10011
USA
enslow.com

Published in 2017 by Enslow Publishing, LLC.
101 W. 23rd Street, Suite 240, New York, NY 10011

Library of Congress Cataloging-in-Publication Data
Names: Ponto, Joanna, author. | Robinson, Fay, author.
Title: Halloween / Joanna Ponto and Fay Robinson.
Description: New York, NY : Enslow Publishing, [2017] | Series: The story of our holidays | Includes bibliographical references and index. | Audience: Grades 4-6.
Identifiers: LCCN 2016001033| ISBN 9780766076525 (library bound) | ISBN 9780766076501 (pbk.) | ISBN 9780766076518 (6-pack)
Subjects: LCSH: Halloween--Juvenile literature.
Classification: LCC GT4965 .P65 2016 | DDC 394.2646--dc23
LC record available at http://lccn.loc.gov/2016001033

Printed in the United States of America

To Our Readers: We have done our best to make sure all websites in this book were active and appropriate when we went to press. However, the author and the publisher have no control over and assume no liability for the material available on those websites or on any websites they may link to. Any comments or suggestions can be sent by e-mail to customerservice@enslow.com.

Portions of this book originally appeared in the book *Halloween: Costumes and Treats on All Hallows' Eve* by Fay Robinson.

Photo Credits: Cover, p. 1 Catherine Delahaye/DigitalVision/Getty Images; p. 4 Eric Cadigan/Shutterstock.com; p. 6 BananaStock/Thinkstock; p. 10 Labrynthe/Shutterstock.com; p. 11 JUSTIN TALLIS/AFP/Getty Images; p. 13 De Agostini/Archivio J. Lange/De Agostini Picture Library/Getty Images; p.14 Private Collection/©Look and Learn/Bridgeman Images; p. 14 © Radharc Images/Alamy Stock Photo; p. 18 GraphicaArtis/Archive Photos/Getty Images; p. 20 Monkey Business Images; p. 22 gpointstudio/iStock/Thinkstock; p. 25 Boston Globe/Getty Images; p. 27 GreenArt Photography/Shutterstock.com; p. 29 © Karen Huang.

Crafts created by Sophie Hayn and Aniya Strickland.

Contents

Halloween is the one time of the year when it is fun to be scared!

Chapter 1

Scary Fun

Imagine that it is dark and spooky outside. Red and yellow leaves blow around on the ground. Other leaves on tree branches move back and forth in the wind. What holiday comes to your mind?

Trick or Treat!

Children put on costumes. They cover their faces with makeup. Some friends arrive. They are all dressed in different costumes. They each have a bag for collecting treats.

They run to a neighbor's house. White threads like cobwebs dangle from the trees. A jack-o'-lantern with a glowing face seems to be watching. Scary music is coming from inside the house.

Everyone likes dressing up as someone else on Halloween. The candy is just a bonus!

One of the children rings the doorbell, and the door slowly opens. The person behind it is ready. "Trick or treat!" everyone shouts. The neighbor smiles and pushes a bowl full of candy toward the group. Each child takes a piece and drops it into his or her bag. What could be more fun?

A Spooky Holiday

Halloween is a time to dress up, be scared in a fun way, and get treats. But where did these customs come from? Why do we wear costumes? Who decided we should be scared in a fun way? And why do we say trick or treat?

The story of this holiday goes back many, many years. As a matter of fact, Halloween is one of our oldest holidays. Just how did it get started?

Chapter 2

Halloween's Howling History

Halloween takes place in autumn. It is a time when the air gets crisp and cool and night sets in early. People stay inside more and spend time with their family.

Long ago, things were different. There were no electric lights, so most activities had to stop when the sun went down. There was no indoor heat. People bundled up and stayed by fires to keep warm. As the leaves fell from trees and plants died, people were frightened. To some, winter seemed like a time of death.

Good and Evil Gods

More than two thousand years ago, a group of people called the Celts (Kelts) lived in Great Britain and Ireland. To explain the things they did not understand, the Celts believed in many gods. Some of the gods were good and some were evil. The sun god was good. The sun gives light and heat. Why did the sun seem to go away as winter came? Would the sun's light come back? The Celts were not sure.

To thank the sun god, they had a day to honor him. This day was the last day of their year—October 31.

This celebration of the sun was mixed with fears about winter. Some stories tell of an evil god who came on this same day. This god, named Samhain (Sow-in), was the god of death. People believed he invited the ghosts of the dead to join him. People did not know what the ghosts might do. People thought the ghosts might enter their

Change of Seasons

In some parts of the country, the weather gets colder and leaves turn colors as they fall off of the trees in October. It was this change in the seasons that may have led to some of the traditions on Halloween.

bodies or the bodies of animals. They thought the ghosts might even pick out who would die in the next year.

Samhain

Because Halloween started so long ago, we cannot be sure what people did or believed then. We must count on the stories people told over time. Some stories say Samhain was a god who caused a lot of trouble on October 31.

Halloween takes place when the sun weakens and the leaves change.

Other stories say there never was a god named Samhain and the word "Samhain" simply means "end of summer." Some stories say ghosts came to earth on their own. People were afraid of these ghosts. They built huge outdoor fires to scare the ghosts away. People wore costumes made of animal skins to frighten the ghosts. They left food outside their homes in hopes that the ghosts would enjoy the food instead of coming inside.

The Celts named this event Samhain after the god who frightened them. It was the beginning of winter and the beginning of Halloween. But there is more to learn about Halloween than that.

People parade through the street on Bonfire Night, a celebration related to Samhain.

Chapter 3

Ghostly Traditions

S amhain is not the only holiday that influenced Halloween. We also get our customs from three other holidays.

Pomona and the Harvest

In about the year 43 CE, a group of people called the Romans took over lands owned by the Celts. The Romans, like the Celts, believed in many gods. One was Pomona, a beautiful maiden. She was the goddess of fruit and orchards. Near November 1, the Romans celebrated Pomona and the harvest with a festival. People gave away gifts of fruits and nuts. They played games and ran races.

All Hallows' Eve

About six hundred years later, the Roman Catholic Church created All Saints' Day to honor their saints. It was first celebrated in the spring. The church later changed the date to November 1, the day after Samhain. The church did not like Samhain because it was not Christian. The church wanted to replace Samhain with a religious holiday. They called it All Hallows, meaning "all saints." The night before was called All Hallows' Eve. This was eventually shortened to Halloween.

All Souls' Day

Around 1000 CE, the church made another holiday called All

The Romans celebrated the goddess Pomona.

People honored their departed loved ones by decorating their graves on All Souls' Day.

Souls' Day, celebrated on November 2. On this day the souls of the dead were remembered. In England on this day, the poor went door to door singing and begging for food at each home. Families would give out money or special cakes called soul cakes. In return, the poor promised to pray for the family members who had died. This activity was called going a-souling.

These holiday traditions have blended together to create our modern Halloween. From Samhain, we get costumes and the idea of a spooky night. From Pomona, we get food and games, such as bobbing for apples. From All Hallows Eve we get the name Halloween. From All Souls' Day, we get going door to door for treats.

Chapter 4

Spooky Symbols

Halloween has a lot of spooky symbols associated with it. Where did we get ideas of witches flying on broomsticks, skeletons, tombstones, and jack-o'-lanterns?

Jack-o'-Turnip?

One Halloween story is about jack-o'-lanterns. Jack was a very bad man, as the story goes. When he died, he could not get into heaven. Even the devil did not want him in hell. So Jack was forced to walk about the earth without a resting place. When Jack complained that he could not see in the dark, the devil threw a glowing coal to him. Jack placed the coal in a turnip and used it as a lantern. The story says that poor Jack is still wandering the earth today.

Before jack-o'-lanterns were carved out of pumpkins, people carved turnips.

The Irish put coals inside turnips on Halloween just like Jack in the story. They carved scary faces on turnips. When the Irish came to America, they used pumpkins instead, which were easier to carve than turnips. Now we do the same thing. It is fun to carve a funny or scary face in a pumpkin. With a flashlight inside, the pumpkin glows just like a lantern.

Bone-Rattling Skeletons

The Celts believed ghosts wandered the earth on Halloween. They also thought ghosts and skeletons danced in graveyards on that night. Ghosts and skeletons are favorite decorations on Halloween today. People also put make-believe tombstones in their yards to make them look like graveyards.

On the night of Samhain, the Celts of long ago wore scary costumes. They wanted to frighten away the ghosts they believed were around. Or, some people say, they wore spooky costumes so the ghosts would think they were already dead. That way, the ghosts would pick on someone else. Now all the real fear is gone from Halloween. We wear scary costumes just for the fun of it.

Wicked Witches

Long ago, people worried a lot about witches. Witches were thought to be ugly and evil. People believed they had magic powers. They could cast spells to cause terrible storms. They could make people sick or turn them into toads. People thought the witches could

Thank the Irish!

Halloween did not become a popular holiday in America until the 1840s, when large numbers of Irish people arrived. The Irish brought many of their customs to the United States, including Halloween.

turn themselves into animals. People blamed witches for bad things they could not explain.

One of the times that witches got together was on Halloween. On that night, it was said that witches would fly through the sky on broomsticks. They would dance and chant around a bonfire.

Today there are still people who call themselves witches. They are not ugly or bad. They just have their own beliefs. Many people believed black cats were witches' pets. Some people even thought

Witches can fly on broomsticks on Halloween.

witches could turn themselves into black cats. Because people were so afraid of witches, they were afraid of black cats, too.

Trick or Treat?

How did the custom of trick-or-treating begin? One explanation comes from Samhain. To keep the ghosts from harming them on this night, the Celts put out treats to keep the ghosts happy. When the poor ate the food, people believed the ghosts had eaten it. If no food was left out, the poor might play a trick. Then people would blame it on the ghosts.

Another story from the Celts tells about a god named Muck Olla. It was said that Muck Olla brought luck and wealth. On Samhain a man wearing a horse costume led the poor from house to house. They told each family to give them gifts for Muck Olla. If the family did not, Muck Olla would bring them bad luck. Most families gave food to the group. If they did not, the poor would play a trick.

Going a-souling on All Souls' Day may also have inspired trick-or-treating. That was when the poor would go door to door begging for food and offering to pray for the souls of the dead.

No matter how it started, going door to door for treats became popular in America in the 1840s.

The phrase "trick or treat" means "give me a treat or I'll play a trick!" But people were going trick-or-treating for one hundred years before they started using those words. It was not until the 1940s that the phrase "trick or treat" was used.

Trick-or-treating is similar to a-souling.

Chapter 5

Hair-Raising Fun

Part of the fun of Halloween is being scared. Sure, ghosts and skeletons are scary. But on Halloween, all these scary things are harmless.

Choose a Costume

Lots of children like to wear scary costumes like the Celts of long ago. Many children dress up as ghosts, jack-o'-lanterns, skeletons, witches, or even black cats. There are other scary costumes, too, such as spiders, bats, vampires, and Frankenstein monsters.

But costumes do not have to be scary. Funny or pretty costumes or costumes of favorite characters are good also.

Costumes can be handmade or store-bought. It is fun to pretend to be someone or something else for one night.

How to Celebrate

All across America, people dress up and do scary things on Halloween. They celebrate in just about the same way everywhere. The only

Bobbing for apples is one fun Halloween activity.

differences are in the kind of parties schools or towns have or whether or not trick-or-treating is done.

Some schools or towns have Halloween parades. Children get to show off their costumes in front of a crowd. After the parade is over, they might get special treats. There might

Is It Fun or Scary?

Halloween might have started out as a scary holiday. But today, we can be scared in a fun, harmless way. Trick-or-treating and going to parties are fun things to do to celebrate Halloween.

be games to play. Or there may be a Halloween dance. Some towns have pumpkin contests. The biggest pumpkin wins. Other towns have scarecrow festivals. People put out scarecrows they make for everyone to see. There might be apple cider, hot cocoa, and different foods made from apples or pumpkins, such as breads, pies, and other treats.

In many places, children go trick-or-treating. The people who answer the door may be wearing a costume, too. They might be playing scary music. But even if they are not in costume, they will have treats.

Some children stay home part of the evening to answer the door. Then they can scare visitors by playing creepy music and dressing in a costume. People usually give away candy for treats. But coins, party favors, small plastic bats, or plastic spiders may also be given.

Throw a Party

Sometimes people have Halloween parties. Here are some ideas to make a great Halloween party.

Turn the lights down low. The dark can make things seem scarier. Make a recording of weird sounds, such as moans, screams, and howls. Rattle sticks to sound like skeleton bones. Play creepy music.

Decorate the party room with spooky things, such as jack-o'-lanterns, tombstones, and skeletons. Use lots of black and orange—they are the colors of Halloween.

Plan to play some games, such as bobbing for apples, pin the tail on the black cat, or musical tombstones. Plan a time for telling ghost stories, too.

Make a hall of horrors. First, put out some "monster parts." Peeled grapes can feel like eyeballs. Gelatin with fruit in it can feel like a monster's guts. A bowl of cooked noodles can feel like brains. You

Adults and kids alike love scaring themselves by walking through frightening haunted houses.

can even make witch finger cookies by following the recipe on page 27. Then, lead kids through the dark, touching the "monster parts" as they go.

Be Safe!

People do not need to be afraid of black cats, ghosts, and skeletons on Halloween, but they should still be careful when they go trick-or-treating. Here are some Halloween safety tips:

- Wear reflective tape on costumes. That way cars can see you in the dark.

- Make sure masks allow clear vision. Makeup is also a good choice.

- Put a flashlights inside jack-o'-lanterns instead of candles.

- Stay on well-lit streets. Cross only at corners.

- Young children should always go trick-or-treating with an adult.

- Have an adult at home check treats before eating them.

Whether trick-or-treating, going to a parade, or having a party, Halloween is all about having a good time.

Witch Finger Cookies*

Ingredients:

2 cups (240 g) all-purpose flour
½ teaspoon (2.5 g) baking powder
¼ teaspoon (1.5 g) salt
(½ cup (120 g) room temperature butter
1 cup (200 g) sugar
1 room temperature egg

1 teaspoon (5 mL) vanilla extract
about 30 whole almonds
1 tube (.75 oz, 22 mL) red decorating gel

Directions:

1. Preheat the oven to 325°F (165° C).
2. In a bowl, mix the flour, baking powder, and salt together with a whisk.
3. In a separate bowl beat the butter and sugar together with an electric beater or stand mixer. In 2 or 3 minutes the mixture should be light and fluffy.
4. Beat the egg and vanilla into the butter and sugar mixture.
5. Continue to beat the butter mixture while you slowly add the flour mixture in small amounts at a time.
6. Chill the dough in the refrigerator for 20 minutes.
7. Grease a baking pan with cooking spray or butter.
8. Scoop out a tablespoonful of the cookie dough at a time. Roll the scoop of dough into a 4- or 5-inch (10–12 cm) finger.
9. Squeeze some red decorating gel onto one end of the finger and then press an almond on top of this. This makes the bloody fingernail!
10. Use the back of a knife to draw lines on the fingers for the knuckles. Take a look at your own fingers to see where these should go. Pinch the dough a little between each knuckle.
11. Repeat this until you have used up all the cookie dough.
12. Bake the cookies for 15–20 minutes, or until they are golden.
13. When the cookies are cool, squeeze some more red gel onto the bottom of the finger so they look like bloody stumps.

* Adult supervision required.

Halloween Craft*

Get into that Halloween spirit! Try making some ghoulish ghosts to decorate and greet trick or treaters.

Here are the supplies you will need:

several pieces of white tissue paper

several small rubber bands

a black marker

string or fishing line

Directions:

1. Take one piece of tissue paper and crumple it into a ball.

2. Lay a second piece of tissue paper flat on a table. Place the balled-up tissue in the center of the flat piece of tissue paper.

3. Pull the flat tissue around the ball and bunch it together. Put a rubber band around the bottom of it. This is the head and neck of the ghost.

4. Draw eyes and a mouth on your ghost with the black marker.

Mini Ghosts

5. Tie a piece of string or fishing line to the rubber band. (Hint: If it is tied to the back of the ghost's head, the ghost will look like it is flying.)

6. Make several ghosts. Tie them to tree branches in your yard or string them around your doorway.

*Safety note: Be sure to ask for help from an adult, if needed, to complete this project.

Glossary

All Saints' Day—A holiday that honors the saints of the Catholic Church.

All Souls' Day—A holiday that honors people who have died.

celebration—A way of observing a holiday or an event.

Celts—A group of people who lived in Great Britain and Ireland more than two thousand years ago and the people who are related to them today.

custom—The way a group of people does something.

decorations—Things people put around their home or office to make it look special.

goddess—A female god.

jack-o'-lantern—A carved pumpkin that is lit up.

saint—Someone who is officially recognized by the church for holiness.

trick-or-treating—Dressing in costume and going door to door for treats on Halloween.

Learn More

Books

Goldsworthy, Kaite. *Halloween.* New York, NY: AV^2 by Weigl, 2012.

Heinrichs, Ann, and Teri Weidner. *Halloween.* Mankato, MN: The Child's World, 2014.

Keogh, Josie, and Eduardo Alamán. *Halloween.* New York, NY: PowerKids Press, 2013.

Marsh, Laura F. *Halloween.* Washington, DC: National Geographic Society, 2012.

Websites

Kids Play and Create
kidsplayandcreate.com/fun-halloween-facts-for-kids-why-do-we-go-trick-or-treating-why-do-we-celebrate-halloween/
Impress your friends with these Halloween tidbits.

***Parents* Magazine: Halloween Crafts**
parents.com/holiday/halloween/crafts/
Have a spooky good time making these Halloween crafts.

Family Education: Halloween Fun and Activities
fun.familyeducation.com/halloween-games/holiday-parties/33353.html
Throw a Halloween party with these ideas, fun facts, and craft projects.

Index